FRANCHISING IN GHANA 2014

Legal and Business Considerations

KENDAL H. TYRE, JR., EXECUTIVE EDITOR
DIANA VILMENAY-HAMMOND, MANAGING EDITOR
COURTNEY L. LINDSAY, II, ASSISTANT EDITOR

LEXNOIR FOUNDATION

FIRST QUARTER 2014

LexNoir Foundation is the charitable, educational arm of LexNoir, an international network of lawyers connecting the African Diaspora.

This publication, *Franchising in Ghana 2014: Legal and Business Considerations*, contains excerpts from *Franchising in Africa 2014: Legal and Business Considerations*. Both works are published by LexNoir Foundation and reflect the points of view of the authors and editors as of the date of publication and do not necessarily represent the opinions, interpretations, or positions of the law firms or organizations with which they are affiliated, nor the opinions, interpretations or positions of LexNoir Foundation or LexNoir.

Nothing contained in this book is to be considered as the rendering of legal advice, either generally or in connection with any specific issues or case. Readers are responsible for obtaining advice from their own legal counsel or other professional. This book, any forms and agreements or other information herein are intended for educational and informational purposes only.

www.lexnoir.org

Table of Contents

Franchising in Ghana

Divine K.D. Letsa and Elizabeth Ashun
Bentsi-Enchill, Letsa & Ankomah

Bibliography of International Franchise Resources

Kendal H. Tyre, Jr., Diana Vilmenay-Hammond, Pierce Haesung Han, Courtney L. Lindsay, II, and Keri McWilliams
Nixon Peabody LLP

Acknowledgment

This book could not have been written without the hard work and dedication of each of the contributing authors and editors. Thank you.

We would like to acknowledge and extend our heartfelt gratitude to Michael Collier and Maria Stallings of the Washington, D.C. office of Nixon Peabody LLP for their invaluable assistance in revising, proofing, and editing this publication.

About the Editors and Authors

Kendal H. Tyre, Jr. – Kendal is a partner in the Washington, D.C. office of Nixon Peabody LLP. He handles domestic and cross-border transactions, including mergers and acquisitions, joint ventures, strategic alliances, licensing, and franchise matters.

In his franchise and licensing practice, Kendal counsels domestic and international franchisors, franchisees, licensors, licensees and distributors regarding U.S. state and federal franchise laws as well as foreign franchise legislation in a variety of jurisdictions. Kendal drafts and provides advice with regard to franchise and license agreements, disclosure documents and area development agreements and has extensive experience drafting and negotiating a variety of other commercial agreements. His client base spans the United States and foreign countries, including South Africa, Kenya, and the United Kingdom.

Kendal is a frequent contributor to franchise publications and a frequent speaker at franchise programs held by the American Bar Association Forum on Franchising and the International Franchise Association.

Kendal is co-chair of the firm's Diversity Action Committee and its Africa Group. Kendal is also the executive director of LexNoir Foundation.

E-mail address: ktyre@nixonpeabody.com

Diana Vilmenay-Hammond – Diana is an attorney in the Washington, D.C. office of Nixon Peabody LLP. She is a member of the firm's Franchise & Distribution Team.

In her franchise practice, Diana works with domestic and international franchisors on transactional and litigation matters. Specifically, she counsels franchisor clients regarding state and federal franchise laws, disclosure and registration obligations.

Diana drafts and negotiates various commercial agreements, including international franchise and development agreements.

Diana has co-authored numerous articles on franchising and frequently co-hosted the Nixon Peabody franchise law webinar series. Topics have included:

- "Franchise Case Law Round-Up: Implications for Your Franchise," February 15, 2012;
- "Social Media Part II: Best Practices in Protecting Your Brand in the New Media," September 14, 2010; and
- "The Awuah Case: Bellwether or Outlier," May 11, 2010

Diana received her J.D. from Howard University School of Law and her B.A. from Georgetown University. She is a member of the American Bar Association (Forum on Franchising).

Email address: dvilmenay@nixonpeabody.com

Pierce Haesung Han – Pierce is an associate in Nixon Peabody's Global Business & Transactions Group. Pierce focuses his practice on three main areas, assisting clients with a variety of complex business transactions.

- Mergers & Acquisitions: Providing assistance to both public and private clients with various mergers and acquisitions, performing due diligence, drafting and negotiating transaction documents, and facilitating closing and post-closing mechanics.
- International Commercial Transactions: Drafting and negotiating a variety of commercial agreements, including international franchise and development agreements, license agreements, and purchase and sale agreements.
- Federal Securities Law Matters: Assisting public and private clients regarding federal securities laws and stock exchange rules relating to corporate governance and disclosure.

Pierce serves as the Secretary of the Asian Pacific Bar Association Educational Fund (an affiliate of the Asian Pacific American Bar Association of the Greater Washington, D.C. Area).

Pierce received his J.D. from Georgetown University Law Center and his B.A. from Case Western Reserve University. He is admitted to practice in the State of New York and the District of Columbia.

E-mail address: phan@nixonpeabody.com

Courtney L. Lindsay, II – Courtney is an associate in Nixon Peabody's Corporate and Finance practice. In his corporate practice, Courtney assists for-profit and non-profit entities with transactional matters and corporate governance. In various capacities, Courtney has been involved in multiple merger and acquisition transactions, including drafting and managing due diligence.

Previously, Courtney worked in the legal and business affairs department at a national cable network, where he handled matters related to the network's LLC agreement, including drafting board and member consent agreements.

Courtney received his J.D. from the University of Virginia School of Law and his B.A. from the University of Virginia. He is admitted to practice in the Commonwealth of Virginia and the District of Columbia.

E-mail address: clindsay@nixonpeabody.com

Keri McWilliams – Keri is an associate in the Franchise & Distribution team of Nixon Peabody LLP. Keri works with clients on a number of franchising issues, including obtaining and maintaining franchise registrations in various states, responding to state inquiries regarding trade practices, ongoing compliance with state and federal regulations, and updating franchise disclosure documents. She also handles franchise sales counseling and franchise system issues.

Keri is a member of the American Bar Association's Forum on Franchising, and the Federal and Minnesota State bar associations. She is also a member of Minnesota Women Lawyers and the Minnesota Association of Black Lawyers, and a volunteer in the Volunteer Lawyers Network.

Keri received her J.D. from the Georgetown University Law Center and her B.F.A. from Washington University. She is admitted to practice in the District of Columbia and Minnesota.

E-mail address: kmcwilliams@nixonpeabody.com

Divine K.D. Letsa – Divine is a partner at Bentsi-Enchill, Letsa & Ankomah in Accra, Ghana. He joined Bentsi-Enchill, Letsa & Ankomah in 1990 and currently leads the firm's Construction, Infrastructure and Transportation practice group. He is active in commercial work for oil companies. His firm has six main practice groups including Construction, Infrastructure and Transportation; Energy and Natural Resources; Litigation and Dispute Resolution, Financial Institutions and Capital Markets, Business and Industry, and Technology, Media and Telecommunications. The firm is the Ghana member of Lex Mundi and Lex Africa.

He received his LL.B from the University of Ghana in 1973 and his law degree from Ghana School of Law in 1975. Prior to joining Bentsi-Enchill, Letsa & Ankomah, Divine was the Assistant Director for Civil Litigation and Legal Advice, Ministry of Justice in Cross River State, Nigeria. Divine was a lecturer for the faculty of law at University of Cross River State. Divine has also served as a legal officer for the State Insurance Corporation of Ghana.

E-mail address: dkdletsa@belonline.org

Elizabeth Ashun – Elizabeth is a Foreign Associate at Bentsi-Enchill Letsa & Ankomah in Accra, Ghana. She relocated to Ghana from the United Kingdom in April 2013 and joined the Construction Infrastructure and Transportation practice group of Bentsi-Enchill Letsa & Ankomah until being called to the Ghana

Bar. Elizabeth is a United Kingdom Qualified Commercial Property Solicitor with over nine years experience in commercial property transactional work with experience in property development, sales and acquisitions, secured lending, corporate assistance and landlord and tenant transactions in the retail, office, industrial and new build residential sectors. Elizabeth has worked in various law firms and also the Public Sector in the United Kingdom.

E-mail address: eashun@belonline.org

About the Book

Franchising in Ghana 2014: Legal and Business Considerations contains excerpts from the larger work, *Franchising in Africa 2014: Legal and Business Considerations*. Both books serve as practical, succinct, easy-to-use reference tools for lawyers, business people and academics to use in navigating the myriad laws and business issues impacting franchise arrangements on the African continent.

This book provides an overview of the franchise industry in Ghana and addresses the typical legal issues confronted when expanding a franchise system in Ghana. The larger work, *Franchising in Africa 2014: Legal and Business Considerations*, covers those laws governing franchising in fifteen other African countries – Angola, Botswana, Burundi, Cape Verde, Democratic Republic of Congo, Egypt, Ethiopia, Ghana, Kenya, Mozambique, Rwanda, South Africa, Tunisia, Zambia and Zimbabwe.

In both books, an author, who is a legal expert in the designated jurisdiction, addresses the basic questions that a franchise lawyer would need to know to competently represent a client in expanding their franchise system to that country.

Each country chapter organizes a discussion of that country's laws under various headings and in a uniform format. Topics were sent to each country's author in the form of a questionnaire, and each author drafted responses to the questions presented. A general overview relating to the political and economic history of the country at the beginning of each chapter provides an initial context for the regulatory framework. [1]

---

[1] The source of information for these sections is the Central Intelligence Agency, https://www.cia.gov/library/publications/the-world-factbook/ (last visited November 3, 2013).

Apart from an overview of the legal framework for franchising, each book contains other articles and resources that should prove useful to those in the franchise industry.

The authors for each chapter are listed at the beginning of a chapter and their biographical information is listed in the previous section, *About the Editors and Authors*.

Readers should always consult with local counsel in the relevant jurisdiction instead of relying solely on the information contained in this book. The laws governing franchising are evolving and local counsel in Ghana are best positioned to provide timely, relevant advice applying the current law to the particular facts of a case.

Franchising in Ghana

Divine K.D. Letsa and Elizabeth Ashun

Bentsi-Enchill, Letsa & Ankomah

Accra, Ghana

Ghana

I.   Introduction

A.   Historical Background of Country

Formed from the merger of the British colony of the Gold Coast and the Togoland trust territory, Ghana on March 6, 1957 became the first sub-Saharan country in colonial Africa to gain its independence. Ghana endured a long series of coups before Lt. Jerry Rawlings took power in 1981 and banned political parties. After approving a new constitution and restoring multiparty politics in 1992, Rawlings won presidential elections for the New Democratic Congress (NDC) in 1992 and 1996, but was constitutionally prevented from running for a third term in 2000. John Kufuor of the New Patriotic Party (NPP) succeeded him and was re-elected in 2004.

John Atta Mills took over as head of state in early 2009. However, he did not complete his term in office due to his untimely death in July 2012 and John Dramani Mahama became the incumbent president.

In the December 2012 elections, the candidates competing for presidency were incumbent President Mahama, his main challenger Nana Akufo-Addo of the NPP, and six other candidates. The Electoral Commission declared President Mahama as the winner. On August 29, 2013, the Supreme Court of Ghana dismissed a petition filed by the NPP challenging the results of the 2012 presidential election, therefore affirming President Mahama as the validly elected president.

B.   Economy of Country

Ghana's economy has been strengthened by a quarter century of relatively sound political stability and management, a competitive business environment and sustained reductions in poverty levels. Ghana is well endowed with natural resources and agriculture accounts for roughly one-quarter of GDP and employs more than half of the workforce, mainly small landholders. The services sector and manufacturing sector

1

accounts for 48% and 26% of GDP respectively. Gold and cocoa production and individual remittances are major sources of foreign exchange.

Ghana opted for debt relief under the IMF Heavily Indebted Poor Country (HIPC) program in 2002, and is also benefiting from the Multilateral Debt Relief Initiative that took effect in 2006. In 2009, Ghana signed a three-year Extended Credit Facility (previously the Poverty Reduction and Growth Facility) with the IMF to improve macroeconomic stability, private sector competitiveness, human resource development, and good governance and civic responsibility. Sound macro-economic management along with high prices for gold and cocoa helped sustain GDP growth between 2008 and 2012.

Ghana successfully completed a five year compact with Millennium Challenge Corporation (MCC), which it signed in 2006. Its goal was to assist in transforming Ghana's infrastructure and agricultural sectors. Ghana is currently in the process of developing a second MCC compact that will focus on the power sector.

Oil production at Ghana's offshore Jubilee field began in mid-December 2010 and has boosted economic growth and crude oil is now Ghana's third main export. President Mahama faces challenges in managing new oil revenue while maintaining fiscal discipline and resisting debt accumulation.

C.   Franchise Legal Overview

There is no specific legislation governing franchising in Ghana and there are also no franchise industry associations in Ghana. Franchise agreements are generally entered into as a result of contractual negotiations between the parties and are therefore regulated by the general principles of contract law. In cases where the franchise will include the provision of specific services such as banking etc., such enterprises will be subject to the regulatory requirements pertaining to that sector.

Ghana

Notwithstanding the foregoing, certain aspects of a franchising agreement may be construed as a transfer of technology and any agreement relating to such a transfer must be submitted for approval and registered with the Ghana Investment Promotion Centre (the "GIPC") pursuant to the *Ghana Investment Promotion Centre Act, 1994 (Act 478)* (the "GIPC Act") and will be governed by the terms of the *Technology Transfer Regulations, 1992 (LI 1547)* ("the TT Regulations").

In July 2013, Ghana's Parliament passed the amended Ghana Investment Promotion Centre (GIPC) Bill 2013 (the "GIPC Bill"), revising the country's investment laws to guarantee optimum business opportunities and incentives for Ghanaian enterprises. The GIPC Bill proposes minor changes to the management of technology transfer agreements. As the GIPC Bill has not yet received Presidential Assent, it is possible amendments to the GIPC Bill may be introduced, debated, and agreed to and further amendments may be made that may affect franchising agreements construed as a transfer of technology.

II.   Regulatory Requirements

A.   Pre-Sale Disclosure

Please describe any pre-sale franchise disclosure or similar requirements that may apply to franchise transactions.

No pre-sale franchise disclosure requirements or similar requirements apply to franchise transactions under the laws of Ghana.

B.   Governmental Approvals, Registrations, Filing Requirements

Please describe any necessary government approvals, registrations, or filing requirements that may apply to franchise transactions.

Ghana

There is no specific legislation under Ghanaian law that requires any government approvals, registrations, or filing requirements for franchise transactions. However, as certain aspects of a franchising agreement may be construed as a transfer of technology, the agreement will be required to be registered with the GIPC[2] and the TT Regulations will apply. Where there is a breach of any of the provisions of the TT Regulations, the GIPC may not register the agreement and the agreement will be considered unenforceable.

Under Section 40 of the GIPC Act, a technology transfer agreement is defined as an agreement relating to an enterprise to which the GIPC Act applies and that involves:

- the assignment, sale or use of foreign patents, trademarks or any other industrial property rights;

- the supply of foreign technical know-how or technological knowledge;

- foreign technical assistance, design and engineering, consultancy or any other technical services in whatever form they may be supplied; and

- foreign managerial, marketing or other services.

However, an agreement will not be regarded as a technology transfer agreement if its duration does not exceed a period of eighteen months.

An enterprise is defined under the GIPC Act as including an industry, a project, an undertaking or a business to which the GIPC Act applies or an expansion of that industry, undertaking, project or business or a part of that industry, undertaking, project

---

[2] The GIPC Bill is proposing that the GIPC shall maintain a record of technology transfer agreements and on receipt of a technology transfer agreement intended for registration shall review the agreement and following registration shall monitor and ensure compliance with the terms and conditions of the agreement.

or business and an enterprise duly registered with the GIPC where there is foreign participation.

For a technology transfer agreement to qualify for registration and not be rendered unenforceable, Regulation 4 of the TT Regulations provides that it must not contain any of the following clauses or contain any clause the effect of which is the same or similar which:

- permit the transfer of technology which is freely and easily available in Ghana; or

- restrict the volume of production or the sale of the franchisee's products in the franchisee's country; or

- completely prohibit the exportation of the franchisee's products or the right to export to specific geographical areas other than to areas where the franchisor has previously granted exclusive rights to third parties; or which require:

  - the franchisee to export exclusively through the franchisor or on unfavorable terms; or

  - the franchisor's prior permission before any export transaction is made; or

  - the franchisee to pay additional royalty on export sales; or

  - an obligation on the franchisee to acquire or procure its inputs including equipment, tools, parts, raw materials or intermediate products exclusively from the franchisor or any other person or a specific source except where such inputs are not commercially available elsewhere or such inputs are special to the technology supplied or are required to meet the specifications of products to be produced either under license or trademark; or

Ghana

> ➤ an obligation on the franchisee to employ personnel to be appointed by the franchisor whose remunerations shall be provided by the franchisee unless in the opinion of the GIPC the obligation is considered indispensable, taking into account the transferred technology; the remuneration for it compares favorably with what prevails in the international market for similar services to be performed by the personnel and in any such case the provisions of the service is supported by a properly drawn-up management or technical services agreement; or

- provide for the obligatory transfer by the franchisee of improvements or innovations introduced or developed, or patents acquired by the franchisee in respect of the licensed technology to the franchisor, except that such a clause, excluding patents acquired by the franchisee, may be permissible where they are mutual or reciprocal; or

- require payment for patent and other industrial property rights after their expiration, termination or invalidation; or

- prohibit the manufacture or sale or both of products based on the technology transferred on the expiration of the agreement, or prohibit the use of licensed technical know-how acquired from the use of the licensed technology after the expiry of the agreement; or

- are designed to prevent the franchisee from contesting or assisting in determining, either administratively or by means of judicial proceedings, the validity of industrial property rights claimed or secured in Ghana by the franchisor; or

- restrict research and development activities of the franchisee to improve and adapt the licensed technology or restrict the franchisee access to continued improvements in techniques and processes related to the licensed technology ; or

- forbid the use by the franchisee of complementary technologies; prevent the manufacture of products different from those covered by the agreement or prevent the manufacture of products similar to those covered by the technology transfer agreement; or

- require the consent of the franchisor before any modifications to products, processes or plants can be effected by the franchisee or which impose on the franchisee obligations to introduce unnecessary designs; except where the licensed technology is used to manufacture specific products under a license or trademark; or

- limit the scope, volume of production or the sale or resale prices of the products manufactured by the franchisee; or

- impose on the franchisee an obligation to sell all its manufactured products to the franchisor at a price fixed by the latter or to any other person or enterprise designated by the franchisor; except that this provision shall not apply where:

  o the franchisee is engaged exclusively in the manufacture of intermediate products, parts or components for subsequent transformation, assembly or finishing by the franchisor, and the franchisor is the sole potential buyer of such intermediate goods; or

  o the requirement is related exclusively to certain export markets; or

- the franchisor can prove that it possesses an adequate distribution system or enjoys sufficient prestige in the trade to be able to market the products covered by the agreement more efficiently than the franchisee provided always that the franchisee shall at all times not be coerced into any such transaction.

It would be advisable that prior to concluding an agreement that bears characteristics of a franchising agreement to seek confirmation from the GIPC whether it constitutes a technology transfer.

C. Limits on Fees and Typical Term of Franchise Agreement

Please describe any limits upon the nature and extent of fees and the term of a typical franchise agreement.

The franchise agreement is a contractual agreement and under Ghanaian law parties are free to enter into any contractual agreement to the extent that the applicable terms and conditions of the agreement are not contrary to Ghanaian law and public policy. There are no specific Ghanaian guidelines on term limits applicable to franchise agreements; therefore, parties are free to indicate the duration of the agreement.

However, for those franchise agreements deemed to be technology transfers, the following applies:

Limits on Nature of Fees

1. Payment for Technology

Royalties in respect of know-how patents and other industrial property rights shall range from 0% to 6% of net sales of the technology recipient.

2. Technical Service/Assistance

Ghana

The fees for technical services or assistance (including know-how) ranges between 0% to 5% of net sales. The fee for know-how must not exceed 2% of net sales. The parties have the option of allowing running or lump sum fees considering the nature of the technical service, its duration and dependence of the franchisee on continued foreign technical expertise – where continuing service is deemed to be required running fees are to be favored.

3.   Management Service Fees

Management fees range between 0% and 2% of profit before tax. The fees for management services of projects for which profit is not anticipated during the early years can range from 0% and 2% of net sales during the first 3-5 years. The level of these fees is reduced pro-rata if the franchisor has 60% or more of the equity share capital of the franchisee company. Where a franchisor provides management/technical services in addition to patent, know-how and trademarks, the total fee shall not exceed 8% of net sales.

Any request for fees higher than the upper levels specified above must be approved by the GIPC.

4.   Taxes on Royalties

Every technology transfer agreement shall provide that taxes due on royalties shall be paid by the franchisor.

Term of a Typical Franchise Agreement

Regulation 9 of the TT Regulations provide that the duration of a technology transfer agreement shall not exceed ten years but it is renewable if required by the parties for subsequent terms each not exceeding five years.[3]

---

[3] The GIPC Bill proposes that a technology transfer agreement may be renewed without the approval of the GIPC and the regulator of the relevant sector but a renewed agreement is subject to registration by the GIPC.

Ghana

III. Currency

If all payments under a franchise agreement must be made in immediately available U.S. Dollars, please advise as to any restrictions, reporting requirements, or regulations concerning the exchange, repatriation, or remittance of U.S. Dollars.

There are no restrictions on the remittance of foreign exchange to or from Ghana; however, all remittances must be made through a person licensed by the Bank of Ghana to carry out the business of money transfers.[4]

Where the franchise is granted to a foreign enterprise, remittance of freely convertible currency is guaranteed and unconditional and can be done though any authorized dealer bank. Section 27(c) of the GIPC Act specifically provides for this in relation to fees and charges in respect of a technology transfer agreement registered under the GIPC Act. Where the franchise agreement relates to operating as a bank, as a non-banking institution engaged in the business of micro-finance etc., or as a credit bureau business, such institutions may be subject to reporting requirements or regulations prescribed by the Bank of Ghana.

IV. Taxes, Tariffs, and Duties

Please do not provide any in-depth comments on tax structuring. However, please provide your general comments on the typical amount of withholding tax that would apply and whether a "gross-up" provision contained in a franchise agreement would be enforceable in your country.

Withholding tax is currently levied as follows for non-residents:

1. Dividend and Interest – 8%[5]

---

[4]   Part III of the *Foreign Exchange Control Act, 2006 (Act 723).*

[5]   Section 85 of *Internal Revenue Act, 2000 (Act 592)*

Ghana

2. Royalties – 15%[6]
3. Management and Technical Service Fees – 15%[7]
4. Payments for goods and services – 15%[8]

This tax exposure can be minimized if the party receiving the payments is incorporated in a country with which Ghana has a double taxation agreement. Currently, double taxation treaties exist between Ghana and the United Kingdom, France, Germany, South Africa, Italy, the Netherlands, Belgium, Switzerland and Nigeria.

Since a franchise agreement is contractual, the rules of contract will apply to any gross-up provision in a franchise agreement and therefore will be enforceable in Ghana in the absence of any contrary intention by the parties.

V. Trademarks

Please advise us as to whether there are any special requirements for granting a valid trademark license, including the use of a registered user agreement or a short trademark license agreement and any required filing of such an agreement with the trademark authorities.

Aside from the requirement under the *Trademarks Act*[9] for the registration of trademarks, no special requirements are necessary for the issuance of a valid trademark license. To that extent, there are no requirements for registered user agreements or short trademark license agreements.

---

[6] Section 85 of *Internal Revenue Act, 2000 (Act 592)*

[7] Section 85 of *Internal Revenue Act, 2000 (Act 592)*

[8] Section 85 of *Internal Revenue Act, 2000 (Act 592)*

[9] *Trademarks Act 2004 (Act 664)*

Ghana

VI. Restrictions on Transfer

Please advise as to whether there are any restrictions (1) on a franchisor to restrict transfers by a master franchisee, any interest in a master franchisee, or the assets of the master franchisee or (2) the ability of a master franchisee to control and/or restrict transfers of a subfranchisee's rights under a master franchise agreement, interest in the subfranchisee, or the assets of the subfranchisee.

A. In Relation to Master Franchisee

Under Ghanaian law, a person may by contract assign a legal right to another person, subject to any contrary intention (express or otherwise) of the parties in the agreement. There is thus no limitation on a franchisor to restrict transfers by a master franchisee, any interest in a master franchisee, or the assets of the master franchisee. The Ghanaian courts have held that an attempt by a third party to interfere with the contractual relations between franchisor and franchisee constitutes the tort of interference with contractual relations.

B. In Relation to Subfranchisees

A person may assign a legal right to another person, subject to any contrary agreement of the parties.[10] The ability of a master franchisee to control and/or restrict transfers of a subfranchisee's rights under a master franchise agreement, transfers of an interest in the subfranchisee, or transfer of the assets of the subfranchisee is therefore not prohibited under Ghanaian law.

VII. Termination

Please advise us as to any laws relating to termination in your country, such as agency laws, required indemnity provisions,

---

[10]   Section 7 of the *Contracts Act, 1960 (Act 25)*.

notice or "good cause" requirements, or other laws affecting termination of a franchise agreement. Please describe.

Given that there is no specific legislation governing franchise agreements in Ghana, a franchise agreement will be governed by the terms and conditions of the franchise agreement. The parties are therefore at liberty to include whatever termination clauses they deem applicable to the contract.

VIII. Governing Law, Jurisdiction, and Dispute Resolution

A.   Choice of Law of Foreign Jurisdiction

Please confirm whether the choice of law of a foreign jurisdiction would likely to be upheld under the law of the country, except for certain matters such as trademarks, bankruptcy, and competition matters, which we assume would be governed by the law in your country.

Under Ghanaian law, an issue arising out of a transaction is determined according to the system of law intended by the parties to the transaction to govern the issue. The Ghanaian courts have held that not only will the choice of law of a foreign jurisdiction be upheld, but consideration will be given to a foreign system of law which the parties may, from the nature or form of the transaction, have intended to govern the issue.[11] However, the Ghanaian courts would also not decline jurisdiction in a matter despite the existence of a choice of law provision if the courts determine that the subject of dispute is closely connected to Ghana.

However, where the agreement is registered with the GIPC as a technology transfer agreement, the laws of Ghana shall govern the agreement[12] and any clause in the agreement that is designed to prevent the franchisee from contesting or assisting in

---

[11] *C.I.L.E v Black Star Line and Another* [1967] GLR 744

[12] Regulation 10 of the *Technology Transfer Regulations, 1992 (LI 1547)*

determining, whether administratively or by means of judicial proceedings, the validity of industrial property rights claimed or secured in Ghana by the franchisor shall be unenforceable.[13]

Where the agreement is registered with the GIPC as a technology transfer agreement, Regulation 11 of the TT Regulations provide that if any dispute cannot be settled amicably, it may be submitted to arbitration:

a) in accordance with the rules of procedure for arbitration of the United Nations Commission on International Trade Law; or

b) within the framework of any bilateral and multilateral agreement on investment protection to which the governments of the franchisor and franchisee are parties; or

c) in accordance with any other international machinery for the settlement of investment disputes agreed to by the parties.

B. International Arbitration Dispute Resolution

Please confirm that a court in your country would honor an election of international arbitration dispute resolution, and therefore refuse to hear any disputes arising under a franchise agreement.

The courts in Ghana will honor an international arbitration agreement. Under Ghanaian law, where a party to an arbitration agreement commences legal proceedings against another party to the agreement in any court, an application may be made to the court to stay the proceedings and the court, if satisfied that there is no sufficient reason why the matter should not be referred in

---

[13] Regulation 4(j) of the *Technology Transfer Regulations 1992 (LI 1574)*

accordance with the agreement, may make an order staying the proceedings. In other words, the determination of whether a stay should be granted is subject to the discretion of the court.[14]

Ghana is a signatory to the *Convention on the Recognition and Enforcement of Foreign Arbitral Awards* (the "New York Convention").

IX.   Non-Competition Provisions

If the franchise agreement prohibits the franchisee from engaging in certain competitive activities during the term of the agreement, and for a 12-month period after the termination or expiration of the agreement, please comment on the enforceability of non-competition covenants in your country.

It is common practice to include non-competition provisions in commercial agreements. The parties in a franchise agreement may freely agree on non-competition provisions, such as the prohibition of the franchise from engaging in certain competitive activities during the term of the agreement and for such reasonable time as the parties may agree after the termination or expiration of the agreement. These prohibitions would be considered enforceable. It is also common to extend the prohibition of competition to affiliates and related persons/ entities of the franchisee. However, as previously noted, as a non-regulated agreement, the parties are free to agree on the existence of a non-competition provision and its terms, always in compliance with general principles of the law.

The competition legislation in Ghana is the *Protection Against Unfair Competition Act, 2000 (Act 589)* (the "Unfair Competition Act") and the general principle, under the Unfair Competition Act, is that a conduct or activity in the ordinary course of industry or commercial activities which is contrary to honest practices is anti-competitive or unfair competition. An activity or conduct includes an act, practice or an omission to

---

[14]   *Khoury v Khoury 1* [1962] GLR 98 at 101 and *C.I.L.E v Black Star Line and Another* [1967] GLR 744 at 747.

act. However, the Unfair Competition Act does not provide a definition of "honest practices".

The Unfair Competition Act does not create any regulatory body or administrative process for the purpose of enforcement. It rather provides that an aggrieved person may seek common law remedies in court. The court may award injunctive, or other equitable remedies, compensatory damages or any other remedy that it deems fit.

Competition is regulated on an industry specific basis and the laws pertaining to some specific industries contain some specific regulations on anti-competitive practices.

However, if the franchise agreement is deemed to be captured by the TT Regulations, the GIPC will not register any agreement which contains any of the anti-competitive clauses referred to in Regulation 4 of the TT Regulations and as mentioned in Section II.B. above.

X.   Language Requirements

Does the law in your country require that a franchise agreement be translated into the local language in order to be enforceable between the parties?

Ghanaian legislation does not require that a franchise agreement be translated into local language for purposes of enforceability; however, in certain instances the parties may be required to produce a certified copy in English, if the franchise agreement is in a language other than English.

Regulation 7 (1) of the TT Regulations provides that it is the duty of the franchisor to give full description of the technology and to supply all necessary documentation and information in English.

Ghana

XI.   Other Significant Matters

Please advise as to whether there are any significant matters not addressed above of which a franchisor should be aware in connection with its entering into a franchise agreement in your country.

It is likely that most franchise agreements exceeding 18 months in duration may be covered by the provisions of the TT Regulations, which in essence favors the franchisee unless suitable contractual alternatives are agreed. Under the TT Regulations, it will be the duty of the franchisor to (i) provide process performance warranties in agreements covering large projects which involve considerable technical complexity not explained to the franchisee at the time of negotiations or before the franchisee makes front-end payments,[15] (ii) guarantee the efficient performance of the technology and the continuous availability of essential spare parts during the tenure of the agreement[16] and (iii) inform the franchisee of improvements and innovations relating to the technology and shall supply them on terms mutually acceptable to the parties[17].

---

[15] Regulation 13 of the *Technology Transfer Regulations 1992 (LI 1574)*

[16] Regulation 7(2) of the *Technology Transfer Regulations 1992 (LI 1574)*

[17] Regulation 7(3) of the *Technology Transfer Regulations 1992 (LI 1574)*

Bibliography of International Franchise Resources

Kendal H. Tyre, Jr., Diana Vilmenay-Hammond, Pierce Haesung Han, Courtney L. Lindsay, II and Keri McWilliams

Nixon Peabody LLP

Washington, D.C.

I. General International Resources

Mark Abell, Gary R. Duvall, and Andrea Oricchio Kirsh, *International Franchise Legislation* B1, ABA FORUM ON FRANCHISING (1996)

Kathleen C. Anderson and Anthony M. Stiegler, *Put Muscle in Your Marks: Enforcing Intellectual Property Rights* W14, ABA FORUM ON FRANCHISING (1995)

Richard M. Asbill and Jane W. LaFranchi, *International Franchise Sales Laws—A Survey* W7, ABA FORUM ON FRANCHISING (2005)

Jeffery A. Brimer, Alison C. McElroy, and John Pratt, *Going International: What Additional Restraints Will You Face?* W4, ABA FORUM ON FRANCHISING (2011)

Michael G. Brennan, Alexander Konigsberg, and Philip F. Zeidman, *Globetrotting: A Workshop on International Franchising* 10/W8, ABA FORUM ON FRANCHISING (1994)

Michael G. Brennan, Alexander Konigsberg, and Philip F. Zeidman, *Globetrotting: Strategies for Launching U.S. Franchisors Abroad* 2/P2, ABA FORUM ON FRANCHISING (1994)

Christopher P. Bussert and Jennifer Dolman, *Regaining Your Trademark After Abandonment or Misappropriation* W7, ABA FORUM ON FRANCHISING (2011)

Ronald T. Coleman and Linda K. Stevens, *Trade Secrets and Confidential Information: Rights and Remedies* W2, ABA FORUM ON FRANCHISING (2000)

Finola Cunningham, *Commerce Department Helps Franchisors Go Global*, in FRANCHISING WORLD 63 (Dec. 2005)

Michael R. Daigle and Alex S. Konigsberg, *Meeting Off-Shore Disclosure and Contract Requirements* F/W13, ABA FORUM ON FRANCHISING (1992)

Jennifer Dolman, Robert A. Lauer, and Lawrence M. Weinberg, *Structuring International Master Franchise Relationships for Success and Responding When Things Go Awry* W22, ABA FORUM ON FRANCHISING (2007)

Gary R. Duvall, Paul Jones, and Jane LaFranchi, *Planning for the International Enforcement of Franchise Agreements* W6, ABA FORUM ON FRANCHISING (1999)

William Edwards, *International Expansion: Do Opportunities Outweigh Challenges?* in FRANCHISING WORLD (February 2008)

George J. Eydt and Stuart Hershman, *Bringing a Foreign Franchise System to the United States* W9, ABA FORUM ON FRANCHISING (2009)

William A. Finkelstein and Louis T. Pirkey, *International Trademarks* W15, ABA FORUM ON FRANCHISING (1991)

William A. Finkelstein, *Protecting Trademarks Internationally: Current Strategies and Developments* B3, ABA FORUM ON FRANCHISING (1996)

Stephen Giles, Lou H. Jones, and Lawrence Weinberg, *Negotiating and Documenting Complex International Franchise Agreements* W21, ABA FORUM ON FRANCHISING (2006)

Steven M. Goldman, Stephen Giles, Marc Israel, and Stanley Wong, *Competition Round Up from Around the World* LB2, ABA FORUM ON FRANCHISING (2004)

David C. Gryce and E. Lynn Perry, *Trademarks and Copyrights in the International Arena* 6/W4, ABA FORUM ON FRANCHISING (1993)

Kenneth S. Kaplan, Andrew P. Loewinger, and Penelope J. Ward, *System Standards in International Franchising* W14, ABA FORUM ON FRANCHISING (2005)

Edward Levitt and Jorge Mondragon, *A Survey of International Legal Traps and How to Avoid Them—Beyond the Franchise Laws* W20, ABA FORUM ON FRANCHISING (2007)

Ned Levitt, Kendal H. Tyre, and Penny Ward, *The Impossible Dream: Controlling Your International Franchise System* W4, ABA FORUM ON FRANCHISING (2010)

Michael K. Lindsey and Andrew P. Loewinger, *International (Non-U.S.) Franchise Disclosure Requirements* W9, ABA FORUM ON FRANCHISING (2002)

Andrew P. Loewinger and John Pratt, *Recent Changes and Trends in International Franchise Laws* W4, ABA FORUM ON FRANCHISING (2008)

Andrew P. Loewinger and Thomas M. Pitegoff, *Avoiding the Long Arm of the Law in International Franchising: Issues and Approaches* W8, ABA FORUM ON FRANCHISING (1995)

Craig J. Madson and Katherine C. Spelman, *Similarity and Confusion in the Intellectual Property Arena* W11, ABA FORUM ON FRANCHISING (1997)

Christopher A. Nowak, John Pratt, and Carl E. Zwisler, *Franchising Internationally with Countries with Opaque Legal Systems* W20, ABA FORUM ON FRANCHISING (2006)

E. Lynn Perry and John L. Sullivan Jr., *Trademark Compliance and Enforcement Techniques* E/W12, ABA FORUM ON FRANCHISING (1992)

Marcel Portmann, *Franchising Sector Proves Global Reach*, in FRANCHISING WORLD (January 2007)

John Pratt and Luiz Henrique O. do Amaral, *Civil Law for Common Law Practitioners (or How to Draft an Agreement for Use Overseas)* W4, ABA FORUM ON FRANCHISING (2002)

Kirk W. Reilly, Robert F. Salkowski and Geoffrey B. Shaw, *Determining the Rules of Engagement in Litigation Here and Abroad* W5, ABA FORUM ON FRANCHISING (2008)

Catherine Riesterer and Frank Zaid, *Basics of International Franchising* L/B2, ABA FORUM ON FRANCHISING (1997)

W. Andrew Scott and Christopher N. Wormald, *Stranger in a Strange Land: Contrasting Franchising in International Expansion* W2, ABA FORUM ON FRANCHISING (2003)

Donald Smith and Erik Wulff, *International Franchising: The Unraveling of an International Franchise Relationship* 15/W13, ABA FORUM ON FRANCHISING (1993)

Frank Zaid, Pamela Mills, and Michael Santa Maria, *Essential Issues in International Franchising* LB/1, ABA FORUM ON FRANCHISING (2001)

II. African Resources

Joyce G. Mazero and J. Perry Maisonneuve, *Franchising in the Middle East and North Africa* W2, ABA FORUM ON FRANCHISING (2009)

Kendal H. Tyre, Jr. and Diana Vilmenay-Hammond, *Franchise World: A Burgeoning Middle Class Spurs Franchise Investment in Africa*, MINORITY BUSINESS ENTREPRENEUR (November 2012)

Kendal H. Tyre, Jr., *IP Protection May Promote Additional Franchise Growth in Africa*, NIXON PEABODY LLP: FRANCHISING BUSINESS & LAW ALERT (September 2012)

Kendal H. Tyre, Jr., *Market Potential for Franchising in Africa*, NIXON PEABODY LLP: FRANCHISING BUSINESS & LAW ALERT (June 2011)

Kendal H. Tyre, Jr. and Courtney L. Lindsay, II, *Continued Growth of Franchising in Africa*, NIXON PEABODY LLP: FRANCHISE LAW ALERT (April 2013)

Kendal H. Tyre, Jr. and Courtney L. Lindsay, II, *Pan African Franchise Federation Holds Inaugural Meeting*, NIXON PEABODY LLP: AFRICA ALERT (June 2013)

Kendal H. Tyre, Jr. and Courtney L. Lindsay, II, *White House Encouraging Private Investment and Transparency in Sub-Saharan Africa*, NIXON PEABODY LLP: AFRICA ALERT (August 2012)

Kendal H. Tyre, Jr. and Diana Vilmenay-Hammond, *African Economic Growth Impacts Franchising on the Continent*, NIXON PEABODY LLP: FRANCHISE LAW ALERT (July 2012)

Kendal H. Tyre, Jr. and Diana Vilmenay-Hammond, *Franchising in Africa*, in FRANCHISING WORLD (August 2013)

John Sotos and Sam Hall, *African Franchising: Cross-Continent Momentum*, in FRANCHISING WORLD (June 2007)

A.   Angola

João Afonso Fialho, *Franchising in Angola*, in FRANCHISING IN AFRICA: LEGAL AND BUSINESS CONSIDERATIONS 91-105 (Kendal H. Tyre, Jr. & Diana Vilmenay-Hammond eds. 2012)

B.   Botswana

Bonzo Makgalemele, *Franchising in Botswana*, in FRANCHISING IN AFRICA: LEGAL AND BUSINESS CONSIDERATIONS 107-117 (Kendal H. Tyre, Jr. & Diana Vilmenay-Hammond eds. 2012)

C.   Cape Verde

João Afonso Fialho, *Franchising in Cape Verde*, in FRANCHISING IN AFRICA: LEGAL AND BUSINESS CONSIDERATIONS 119-132 (Kendal H. Tyre, Jr. & Diana Vilmenay-Hammond eds. 2012)

D.   Egypt

Girgis Abd El-Shahid, *Franchising in Eqypt*, in FRANCHISING IN AFRICA: LEGAL AND BUSINESS CONSIDERATIONS 133-142 (Kendal H. Tyre, Jr. & Diana Vilmenay-Hammond eds. 2012)

A. Safaa El Din El Oteifi, *Egypt*, in INTERNATIONAL FRANCHISING EGY/1 (Dennis Campbell gen. ed. 2011)

E.   Ethiopia

Yohannes Assefa and Biset Beyene Molla, *Franchising in Ethiopia*, in FRANCHISING IN AFRICA: LEGAL AND BUSINESS CONSIDERATIONS 143-157 (Kendal H. Tyre, Jr. & Diana Vilmenay-Hammond eds. 2012)

Kendal H. Tyre, Jr., Yohannes Assefa and Getachew Mengistie Alemu, *New Intellectual Property Regulation Requires Scramble to Protect Marks in Ethiopia*, NIXON PEABODY LLP: AFRICA ALERT (October 2013)

F.   Ghana

Divine K.D. Letsa and Hawa Tejansie Ajei, *Franchising in Ghana*, in FRANCHISING IN AFRICA: LEGAL AND BUSINESS CONSIDERATIONS 159-167 (Kendal H. Tyre, Jr. & Diana Vilmenay-Hammond eds. 2012)

G.   Libya

Kendal H. Tyre, Jr. & Diana Vilmenay-Hammond, *First U.S. Franchise Opens in Libya*, NIXON PEABODY LLP: AFRICA ALERT (August 2012)

H.   Mozambique

Diogo Xavier da Cunha, *Franchising in Mozambique*, in FRANCHISING IN AFRICA: LEGAL AND BUSINESS CONSIDERATIONS 169-182 (Kendal H. Tyre, Jr. & Diana Vilmenay-Hammond eds. 2012)

I.   Nigeria

Theo Emuwa and Bimbola Fowler-Ekar, *Franchising in Nigeria*, in FRANCHISING IN AFRICA: LEGAL AND BUSINESS CONSIDERATIONS 183-198 (Kendal H. Tyre, Jr. & Diana Vilmenay-Hammond eds. 2012)

Kendal H. Tyre, Jr. and Theo Emuwa, *Nigerian Franchising: Making Your Way Through the Thicket*, NIXON PEABODY LLP: FRANCHISE LAW ALERT (June 2005)

J.   South Africa

Eugene Honey, *Franchising and the New Consumer Protection Bill*, BOWMAN GILFILLAN (March 2008)

Eugene Honey, *Franchising and the Consumer Protection Bill*, BOWMAN GILFILLAN (May 2008)

Eugene Honey, *Pitfalls and Difficulties with the CPA*, ADAMS & ADAMS (March 2013)

Eugene Honey, *Disclosure is Compulsory*, ADAMS & ADAMS (May 2013)

Eugene Honey and Wim Alberts, *Fundamental Consumer Rights: The Right to Equality*, BOWMAN GILFILLAN (March 2009)

Eugene Honey and Wim Alberts, *The Reach of the Consumer Protection Bill: The Final*, BOWMAN GILFILLAN (March 2009)

Eugene Honey, *South Africa*, in GETTING THE DEAL THROUGH: FRANCHISE (2013) 172-178 (Philip F. Zeidman ed. 2013)

Taswell Papier, *Franchising in South Africa*, in FRANCHISING IN AFRICA: LEGAL AND BUSINESS CONSIDERATIONS 199-224 (Kendal H. Tyre, Jr. & Diana Vilmenay-Hammond eds. 2012)

Kendal H. Tyre, Jr., *A New Legal Landscape for Franchising in South Africa*, NIXON PEABODY LLP: FRANCHISING BUSINESS & LAW ALERT (September 2009)

K.   Tunisia

Yessine Ferah, *Franchising in Tunisia*, in FRANCHISING IN AFRICA: LEGAL AND BUSINESS CONSIDERATIONS 225-245 (Kendal H. Tyre, Jr. & Diana Vilmenay-Hammond eds. 2012)

Kendal H. Tyre, Jr., Diana Vilmenay-Hammond, and Yessine Ferah, *New Franchise Legislation in Tunisia*, NIXON PEABODY LLP: FRANCHISE LAW ALERT (September 2010)

L.   Zambia

Mabvuto Sakala, *Franchising in Zambia*, in FRANCHISING IN AFRICA: LEGAL AND BUSINESS CONSIDERATIONS 247-255 (Kendal H. Tyre, Jr. & Diana Vilmenay-Hammond eds. 2012)

14768142.1

www.ingramcontent.com/pod-product-compliance
Lightning Source LLC
Chambersburg PA
CBHW060450240326
41598CB00088B/4421